Reproduci *for Early Learners!*

Little Kids... TRACE!

Large Tracing Patterns for Developing Cognitive and Fine Motor Skills!

Written and Illustrated by:
Karen Sevaly
Contributing Editor:
Libby Perez
Graphic Designer:
Cory Jackson

Look for All of Our
Little Kids... books
at your local educational retailer!

Table of Contents

Copyright © 2000

Teacher's Friend, a Scholastic Company.

All rights reserved.

Printed in China.

ISBN-13 978-0-439-50410-2

ISBN-10 0-439-50410-4

Safety Warning! The activities and patterns in this book are appropriate for children age 3 to 6 years old. It is important that children only use materials and products labeled child-saf and non-toxic. Remember that young children should always be supervised by a competent adu and youngsters must never be allowed to put small objects or art materials in their mouths Please consult the manufacturer's safety warnings on all materials and equipment used wit young children.

Little Kids... Books!

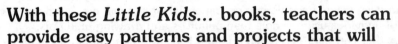

Welcome to the wonderful world of
young learners where play is learning
and learning is fun!

With these *Little Kids...* books, teachers can
provide easy patterns and projects that will
help young children obtain the necessary skills needed for their development.
The simple activities of cutting, tracing, coloring and pasting provide a variety
of cognitive learning skills that will help prepare young learners for reading
and writing. These important developmental skills consist of:

Fine Motor Skills
> finger-wrist dexterity, arm-hand movement, hand-eye coordination

Perceptual Motor Skills
> identification, color and shape recognition, matching and location,
> spatial relationships

Expressive and Receptive Language Skills
> listening, speaking, questioning, relating words and pictures,
> imitation, utilization, recognition and discrimination, visual
> perception and discrimination

Social and Emotional Skills
> creativity and imagination, pride in accomplishments, self-reliance,
> self-control, self-confidence

The early years of schooling helps determine how a child will learn for a life-
time. During this period, children develop a sense of self and decide whether
school is a burden or a joy. We hope these books assist you in your goal to
provide each child with a fulfilling and fun learning experience!

Introduction

Little Kids...Trace!

Small children need to be able to successfully trace simple lines and shapes before they can learn to write numbers and letters. They also need to be able to identify the numbers and letters of the alphabet by their shapes and forms. During this time, youngsters also need to begin to understand the principle that letters have sounds and that these sounds make words. It is important that you provide activities and experiences to teach both phonemic awareness and basic writing skills. You should motivate the children with a print-rich environment and have materials and manipulatives available to help you teach these essential concepts.

The tracing patterns in this book will help preschoolers develop the fine and perceptual motor skills they will need for beginning writing. However, before a youngster can even trace a simple line on paper, he or she will need to develop some fine motor skills by participating in a variety of activities using simple manipulatives and drawing materials. Below, you will find a few simple ideas and activities that can help you teach a young learner how to hold and manipulate a pencil. These activities will also help give the child the practice he or she needs to draw and make basic strokes. Introduce the first few tracing pages found in this book only after the child masters these simple activities.

MANIPULATIVES FOR COORDINATION - Have young children manipulate a variety of simple household items to help develop hand-eye coordination and fine motor skills. Here are some examples:
- Screw lids on and off jars and containers
- Use a hole punch on colorful paper
- Pick up small objects with a pair of tweezers
- Assemble large puzzle pieces
- Unbutton and button large buttons
- Clip clothespins to the edge of a cardboard box
- String large beads
- Put pegs in a pegboard
- Snip paper with a pair of child-safe scissors
- Insert a key to unlock a lock or door

HOLDING A PENCIL/CRAYON CORRECTLY - Young children will naturally tend to hold a crayon or pencil in their fist. Gently show children that they will have more control if they hold the pencil in their fingers, as shown in the illustration (right). You may find that each child holds a pencil in a way that best fits his or her hand naturally. (Remember, some children have short fingers and others have long ones.) Simply encourage a balanced, relaxed grip. Very young children may tend to use either hand when first drawing. Usually by five years old, the dominant hand is well established. Authorities agree that there is no merit in attempting to make a left-handed child use his or her right hand.

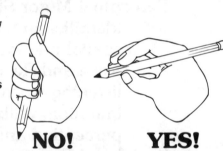

NO!   **YES!**

FIRST TIME DRAWING ACTIVITIES - Before children can trace a given line, they need experience at simple freehand drawing. You will find that youngsters love to draw and experiment with different writing tools, colors and surfaces. Here are some fun suggestions that will enhance their development:
- Have each child draw using large crayons (with paper peeled away) on an extra large sheet of butcher paper taped to the classroom floor.
- Instead of asking children to draw specific items, ask them to draw something happy, funny, pretty, etc. Encourage the children to be creative and to express themselves.
- Have students practice drawing on a vertical surface by attaching a large sheet of paper to an easel, wall, door or outside fence. This will enable them to exercise the muscles in their fingers and hands in a different way.
- Provide a sand table or large dishpan filled with clean sand and have students draw designs and shapes using their fingers or plastic utensils. (You may want to add water to the sand and have the children draw in wet sand as well.)
- On a warm, sunny day, give students a cup of clean water and a paint brush and encourage them to draw on the sidewalk or block wall. Add a few drops of food coloring to the water, if you wish.
- Place several dollops of shaving cream on a cookie sheet. Have the child smooth out the shaving cream and then draw in the cream with a pointed index finger.
- You can also cover a cookie sheet with chocolate pudding. Make sure the child has clean hands before drawing the designs and instruct him or her to not lick their fingers until after the exercise.
- Cover an 8-inch square of cardboard with aluminum foil and have the child draw on the foil using a blunt pencil or craft stick.

Note: Before using the tracing patterns in this book, make sure the children understand that they are to follow the direction of the arrows indicated on the pages. To illustrate the significance of the arrows you may want to draw arrows in four directions on the chalkboard--right, left, up and down. Have students point in the direction each arrow points. Children can also draw a chalk line from the arrow on the board to the direction in which it points.

FIRST TIME TRACING ACTIVITIES - After students have practiced drawing on their own, you can begin introducing them to the patterns in this book.   Here are a few helpful tracing hints:

- **Crayons, Not Pencils** - Have the children use crayons rather than pencils.
  Large crayons with the paper removed are easier for small hands to hold and manipulate.
- **Rainbow Tracing or Writing** - Have the children "rainbow write" by having them trace each pattern several times using a different color crayon for each tracing. This will give the child more practice and enable you to see how many times the pattern was been traced.
- **Straight, Vertical Lines** - Begin with these lines and have the child start at the top and trace down.
- **Left to Right Tracing** - Always have the child trace left to right when tracing all horizontal lines. This will give them practice at moving their eyes and hands in the same direction as words are written.
- **Shapes** - By drawing shapes, children can begin to draw objects rather than just squiggles. Remember, before a child can write the letters of the alphabet, he or she needs to be able to draw simple, basic shapes.

Many children begin writing some letters and numbers before kindergarten. If this is the case, parents should make sure that the child is taught to form the letters the same way they will when they learn to write in school. The first word the child should be taught to write is his or her name. Make sure you teach the beginning letter in uppercase and the remaining letters in lowercase. You also need to make sure that the child is ready to learn to write before you begin any instruction. A child's desire to write is one criterion by which to judge his or her readiness. It is also essential that the child has demonstrated sufficient eye, hand and arm control before he or she can manipulate pencil and paper.

LETTER AND NUMBER TRACING AND WRITING - Before children actually begin tracing and writing numbers and letters with pencil and paper, introduce some of these fun kinesthetic (finger tracing) activities:

- On a vertical surface, such as a wall or door, use strips of masking tape to form the letter you wish to teach. Have the child trace the tape letters so that he or she can learn how the letter if formed.
- Cut letters from sandpaper or felt and have the children trace the letters.
- Glue yarn to a square of posterboard to form an uppercase or lowercase letter. Let the glue dry overnight and then have students trace the selected letter.
- After the children have learned how to form the selected letter, have them trace it in the air as they follow your lead. A simple "fingerplay" or rhyme about the selected letter will help each child remember what the letter looks like and how it is written.
- Trace the selected letter on the child's back and see if he or she can recognize the letter. Have them trace the same letter on your back.
- Draw simple shapes or lines on a plain piece of paper. Staple the sheet on top of a sheet of carbon paper with another sheet of paper. Have the child trace the shapes on the top sheet with a sharp pencil or ballpoint pen. Have the child lift the top papers to see the copied shapes on the bottom sheet.

You may have questions as to which letters to introduce first. Many teachers recommend starting with the first letter of the child's name. Most introduce the uppercase letters first followed by the lowercase ones. In many cases, success is often achieved by teaching the consonant letters first and then the vowels. However, sometimes teachers simply begin with the letter "A" and proceed in order through the alphabet. Consult your school's adopted curriculum or excepted standards in determining your teaching method.   Here are a few more hints and ideas:

- It is important that you demonstrate the proper way to write each letter. Do this several times before you have the child attempt to trace the letter. Show each of your strokes in the same way each time you write the letter.
- The tracing letters and numbers found in this book have arrows that show you how to correctly print each one. (Letters and numbers are represented in simple manuscript style.) Start at the number one arrow and make the strokes in order, tracing over the dotted lines.
- As the child gains confidence in his or her tracing abilities, have the child try writing the individual letters without tracing. Make sure they continue to use the proper strokes in the correct order.
- Have the children use oversized pencils or pencils with "pencil grips." Provide plain paper when children are first learning to write letters. (Young children often have difficulty staying within the lines of lined paper.)
When they are ready for lined paper, use primary writing paper with lines of no less than 1 inch (2.5cm) apart.
- Instruct each child to place the paper straight up-and-down on the desk or table top. (Slant the paper to the left only for teaching traditional cursive or modern manuscript.) Children should sit in an appropriately sized chair that has a straight back.
- After each new letter has been introduced to the class, use a center activity to reinforce good handwriting skills. Stock a center with manuscript paper, pencils, crayons and construction paper sheets with the new letter written on them. Students should use a variety of crayons to trace the letter several times before practicing the letter on handwriting paper.

I can trace !

_____

Name _____

Teacher _____   Date _____

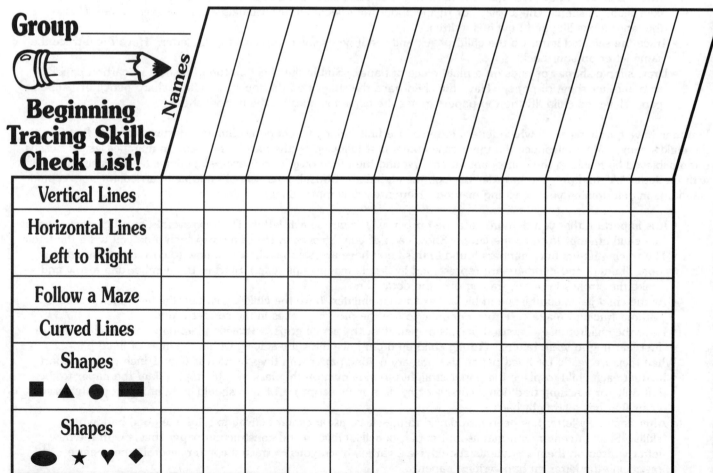

Group _____

Beginning Tracing Skills Check List!

Names									
Vertical Lines									
Horizontal Lines Left to Right									
Follow a Maze									
Curved Lines									
Shapes ■ ▲ ● ▬									
Shapes ⬬ ★ ♥ ◆									

Beginning Tracing Skills Check List!

Names

Short Lines									
Circles									
A a									
B b									
C c									
D d									
E e									
F f									
G g									
H h									
I i									
J j									
K k									
L l									
M m									
N n									
O o									
P p									
Q q									
R r									
S s									
T t									
U u									
V v									
W w									
X x									
Y y									
Z z									
Trace Numbers 1-10									
Trace Name									

Trace the lines to connect the spiders to the web. Use "rainbow tracing." Color the picture.

ace from left to right. Use "rainbow tracing."
Color the pictures.

© Teacher's Friend, a Scholastic Company

TF1453 Little Kids...Trace!

Trace the lines to match the animal to their treat. Use "rainbow tracing." Color the pictures

10

TF1453 Little Kids...Trac

Trace the lines left to right.

TF1453 Little Kids...Trace!

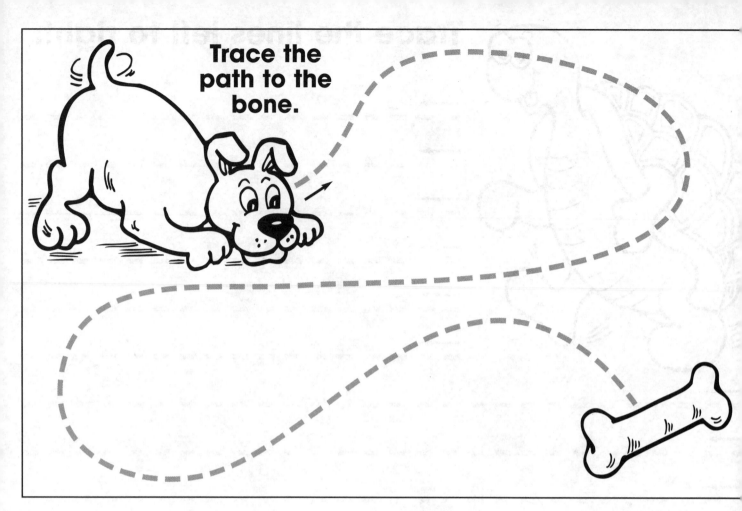

Trace the path to the bone.

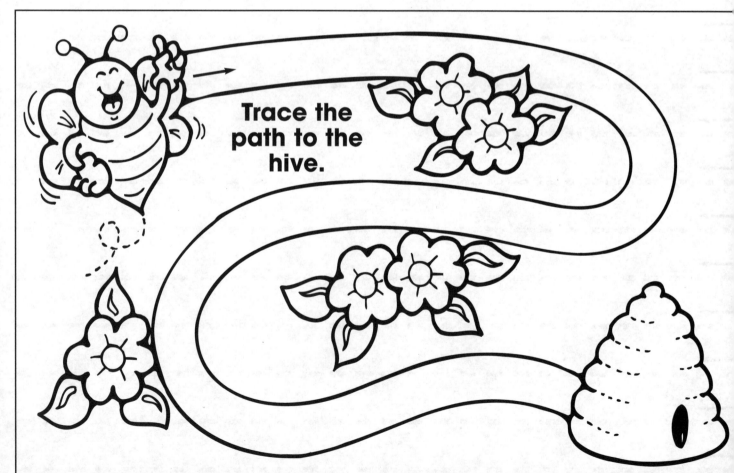

Trace the path to the hive.

TF1453 Little Kids...Trac

Help the elephant get to the circus!

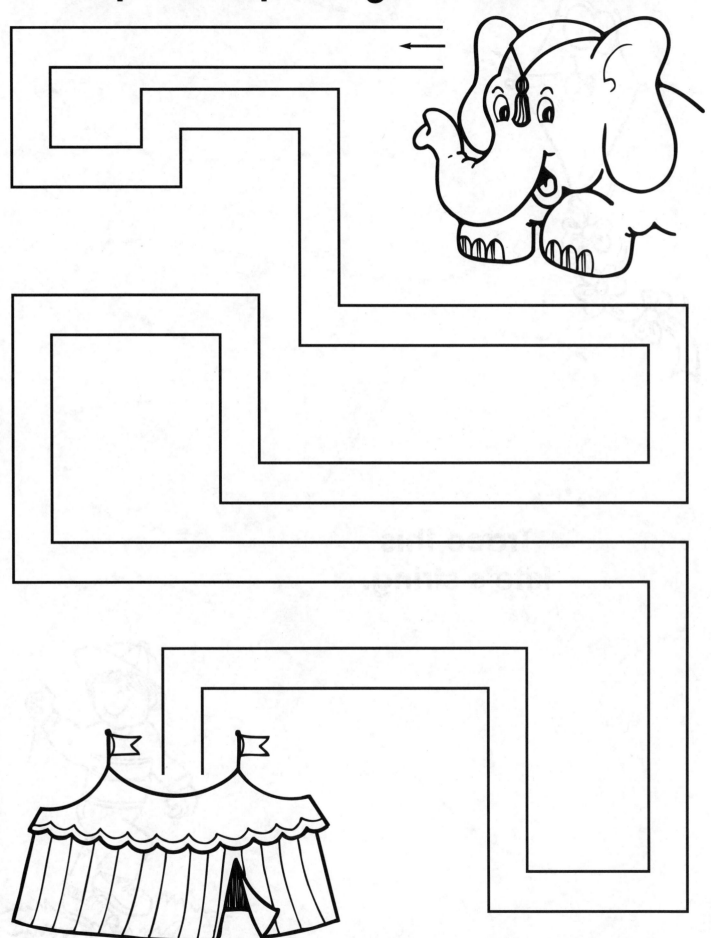

Trace this kite's string.

14

Trace the paths of these butterflies.

TF1453 Little Kids...Trace!

Trace these lines.

Trace these waves.

Trace this rainbow.

Trace these lines.

TF1453 Little Kids...Trac

Trace these shapes and then color.

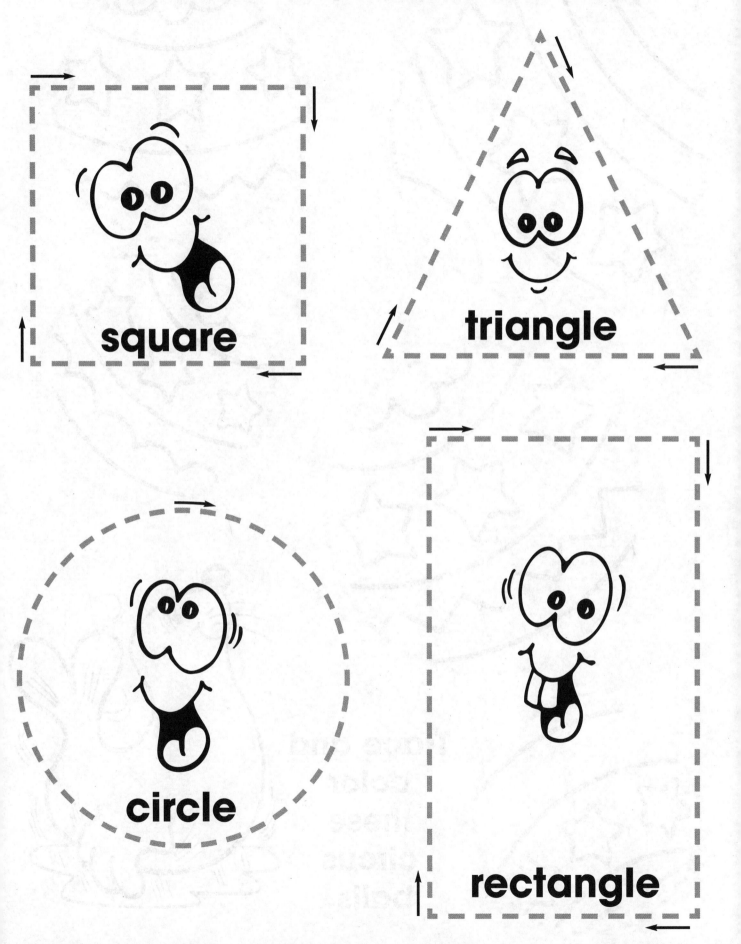

square

triangle

circle

rectangle

19

TF1453 Little Kids...Trace!

Trace and color these circus balls.

Trace and color these squares.

Trace and color these triangles.

Trace and color these rectangles.

Trace and color these shapes.

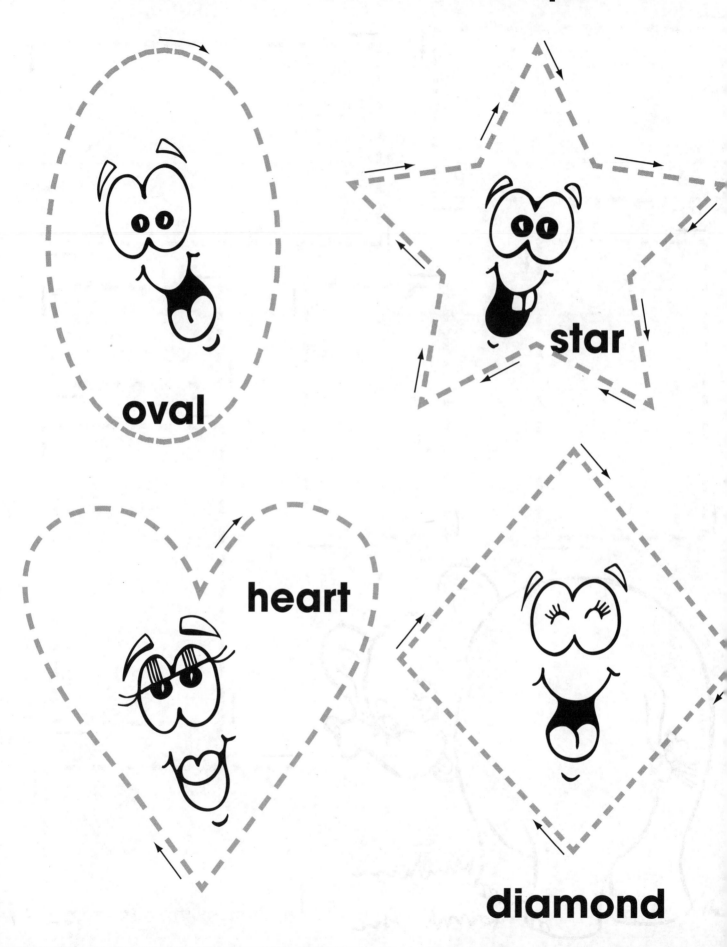

oval

star

heart

diamond

Trace and color these ovals.

TF1453 Little Kids...Trace!

Trace and color these diamonds.

Trace and color these stars.

Trace and color these hearts.

TF1453 Little Kids...Trace

Trace these circles and ovals.

TF1453 Little Kids...Trace!

Trace these lines and circles.

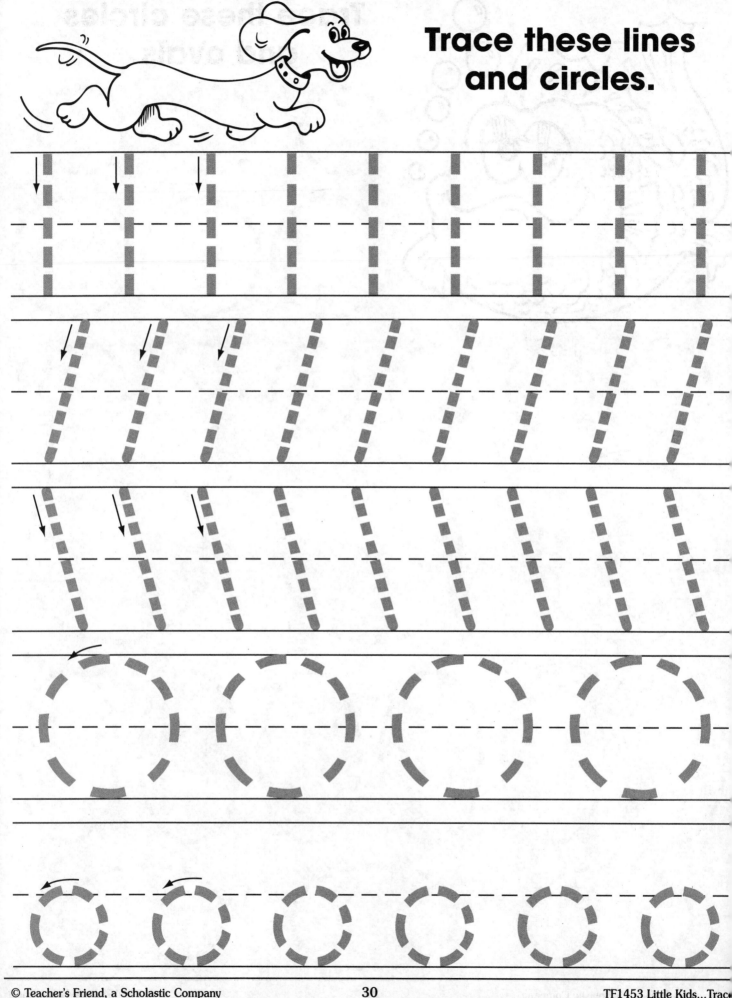

TF1453 Little Kids...Trace

Trace these letters.

A a

B b

Trace these letters.

Trace these letters.

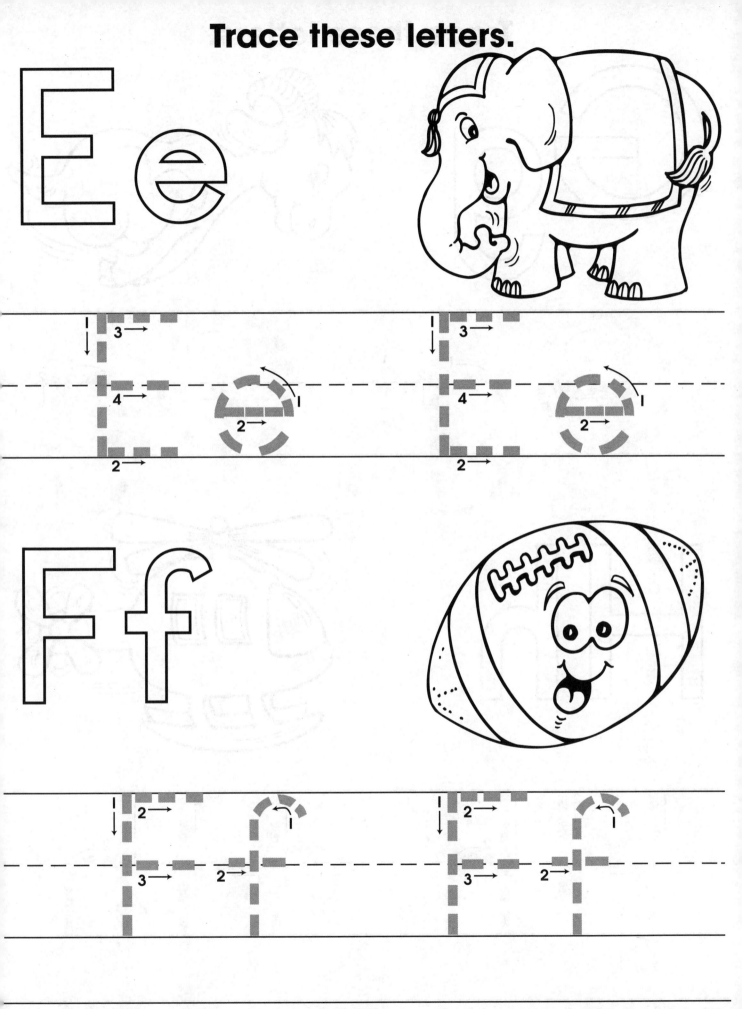

Trace these letters.

Trace these letters.

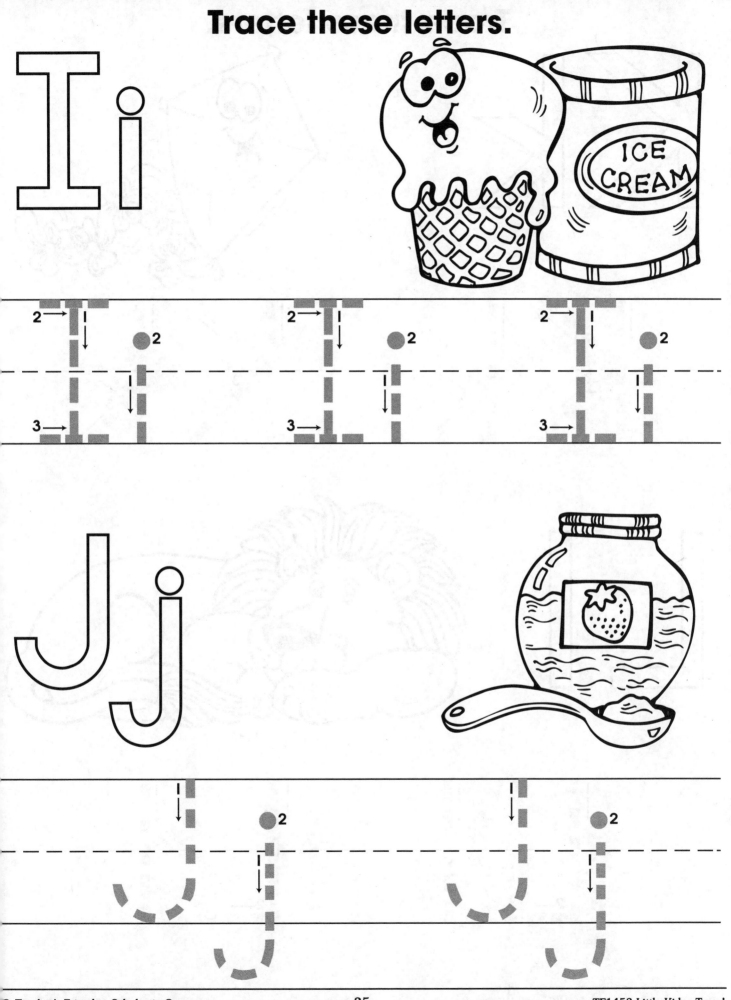

I i

J j

ICE CREAM

Trace these letters.

K k

L l

Trace these letters.

Trace these letters.

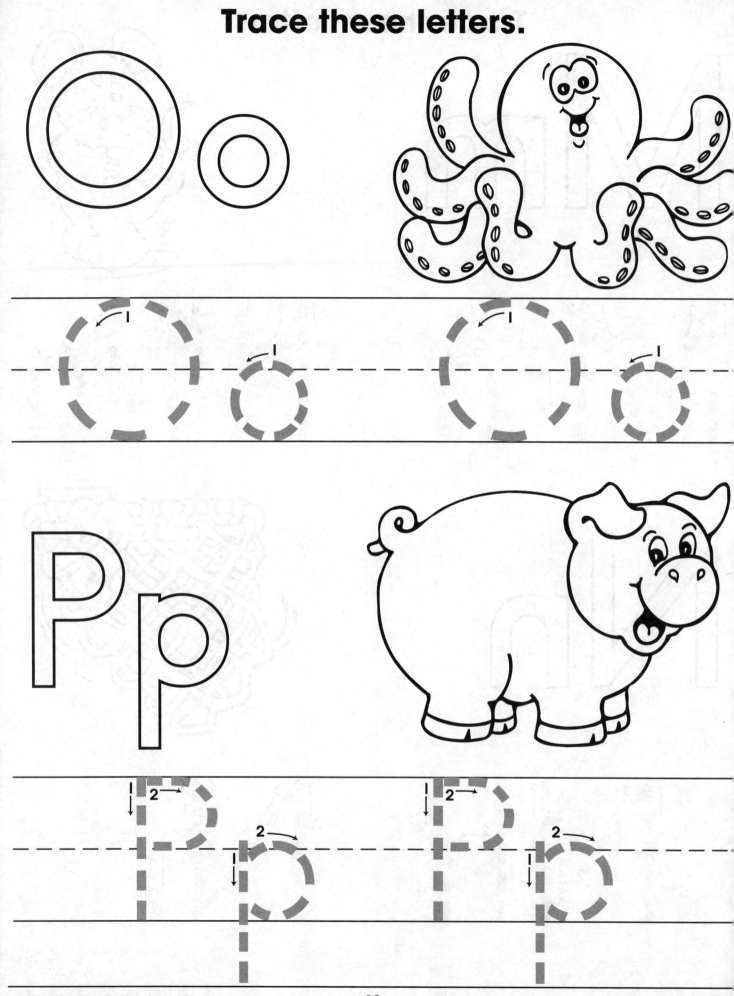

Trace these letters.

Q q

R r

Trace these letters.

S s

T t

Trace these letters.

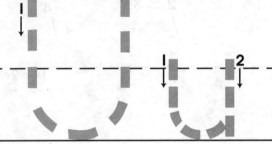

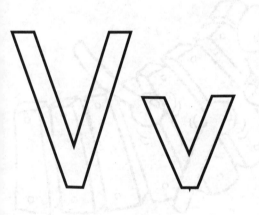

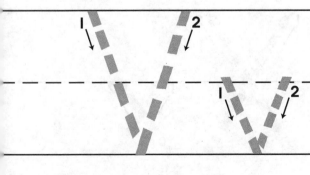

Trace these letters.

W w

X x

Trace these letters.

TF1453 Little Kids...Trace!

Trace the Number One!

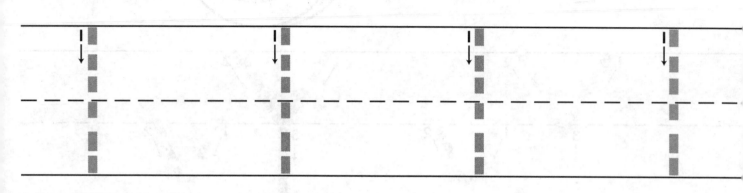

Trace the Number Two!

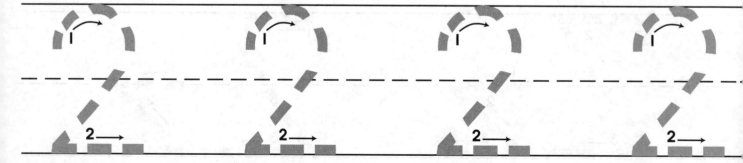

Trace the Number Three!

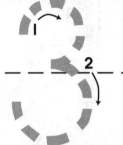 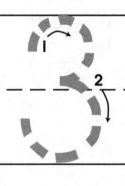 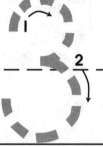

Trace the Number Four!

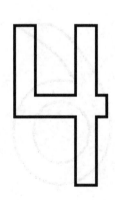

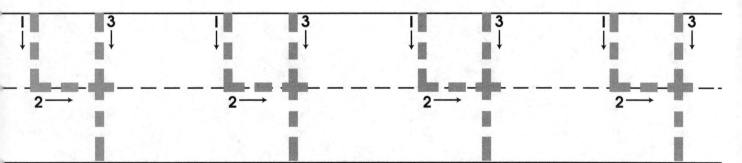

Trace the Number Five!

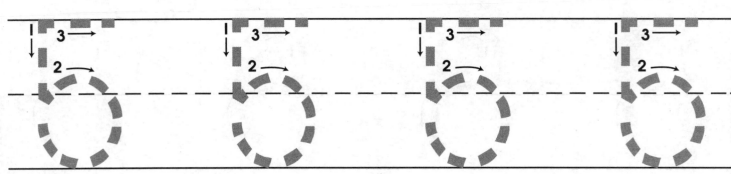

Trace the Number Six!

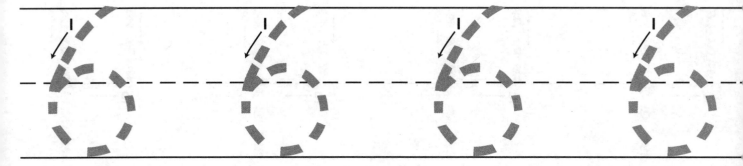

Trace the Number Seven!

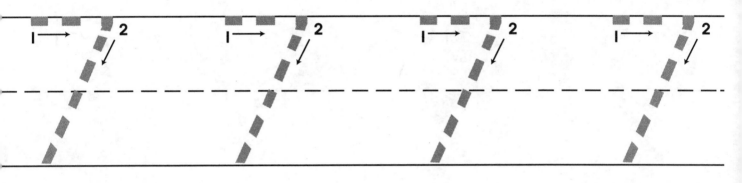

Trace the Number Eight!

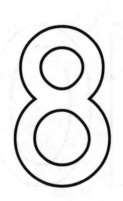

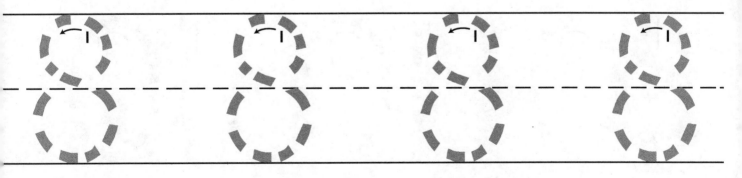

Trace the Number Nine!

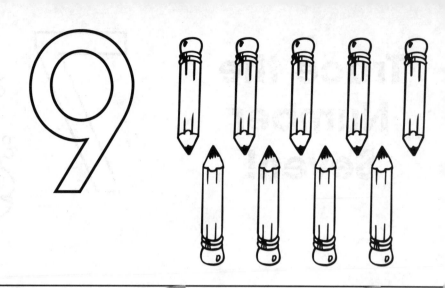

Trace the Number Ten!